About the Author

(May not be a photographic likeness)

Ben Brusey likes to eat food at restaurants when he can. He also likes to compete in eating challenges and his record is thirty fish fingers in one sitting (plus mayo, lemon and ketchup). His favourite restaurant in London is the *Phât Phúc Noodle Bar*, located near South Kensington. 'Phât Phúc' translates as 'Happy Buddha'. Seriously.

PU PU HOT POT
THE WORLD'S BEST RESTAURANT NAMES

BEN BRUSEY

VIKING
AN IMPRINT OF PENGUIN BOOKS

VIKING

Published by the Penguin Group
Penguin Books Ltd, 80 Strand, London WC2R 0RL, England
Penguin Group (USA) Inc., 375 Hudson Street, New York, New York 10014, USA
Penguin Group (Canada), 90 Eglinton Avenue East, Suite 700, Toronto, Ontario, Canada M4P 2Y3
(a division of Pearson Penguin Canada Inc.)
Penguin Ireland, 25 St Stephen's Green, Dublin 2, Ireland (a division of Penguin Books Ltd)
Penguin Group (Australia), 250 Camberwell Road,
Camberwell, Victoria 3124, Australia (a division of Pearson Australia Group Pty Ltd)
Penguin Books India Pvt Ltd, 11 Community Centre,
Panchsheel Park, New Delhi – 110 017, India
Penguin Group (NZ), 67 Apollo Drive, Rosedale, Auckland 0632, New Zealand
(a division of Pearson New Zealand Ltd)
Penguin Books (South Africa) (Pty) Ltd, Block D, Rosebank Office Park,
181 Jan Smuts Avenue, Parktown North, Gauteng 2193, South Africa

Penguin Books Ltd, Registered Offices: 80 Strand, London WC2R 0RL, England

www.penguin.com

First published 2012
001

Colour reproduction by Altaimage Ltd
Printed in China

A CIP catalogue record for this book is available from the British Library

ISBN: 978-0-670-92182-9

ALWAYS LEARNING   **PEARSON**

For Lily Faber. Without whom this book would have been so much classier

CONTENTS

A Taste for Pu Pu

For too long, restaurants have been judged on the quality of their food. In some parts of the world, chefs have been known to waste literally hours of their lives carefully preparing and cooking stuff, only for other people to eat it and, later, part ways with it. This insanity must stop. There is only one thing to look for in a restaurant; a secret hidden in the pages you are about to read or, perhaps, devour.

In buying and using this guide (and it is a guide) you are choosing Man's mastery of language over linguine, smile over sustenance. We have scoured the globe, from Sunderland to Majorca, to find the world's best-named restaurants, bars and cafés. Breathtaking discoveries have been made; new standards of culinary excellence have been set. So cancel that table at the Ritz, forget that drink at the Savoy, and open wide for a mouthful of wisdom guaranteed to leave you hungry, thirsty and gagging for more.

Ben Brusey
(GCSE in Food Technology)

Kebabs especially for you.
Or to share with neighbours

Roaming, UK

You know what they say about restaurants with big plates . . .

Edinburgh, UK

2-for-1 on Back to Black label vodka

Sunderland, UK

Cod is a DJ

London, UK

Sister store to Sell Fridges

London, UK

Spice that rubs you up the wrong way

London, UK

'Phât Phúc' translates as 'Happy Buddha'. Seriously

PHẬT PHÚC
NOODLE BAR

Authentic Vietnamese
Noodle Soup

London, UK

Eating with the fishes

London, UK

You'll be bowled over

London, UK

*'Piggie Piggie Piggie, can't you see
Sometimes your baps just hypnotize me'*

THE NOTORIOUS
P.I.G
OUR FAMOUS SANDWICH...
Southern Style pulled pork
Served W. Anna Mae's
homemade BBQ sauce.
£5.50

London, UK

Get your vines off me,
you damned dirty grapes!

London, UK

Previously 'The Gill Next Door'

Sheffield, UK

Not Vajayjay

London, UK

Tired mochas, washed-up espressos

Edinburgh, UK

The best sausage sandwiches around

London, UK

Getting to know you! . . . over Pad Thai

The King and Thai

Authentic Thai Cuisine

Upper Floor, 33A High Street, Ironbridge, Shropshire
Tel: 01952 433913

Entrance ⟶

Shropshire, UK

*Come for the steak,
stay for the company*

Kent, UK

Fish are food, not friends

Goole, UK

Pull the Donner from the hat

Dublin, Ireland

Full of fresh aromas

Grasse, France

That's the last time I'll eat there!

Berlin, Germany

Knock Knock!

Who's there?

Falafel

Falafel who?

Falafel off his bike and hurt his knee!

London, UK

*'Food with passion
to get your pulse racing'*

XXX Review

Budapest, Hungary

Food to die for

Budapest, Hungary

'Darkly atmospheric'

Anonymous customer review

London, UK

'Call me Fishmael'

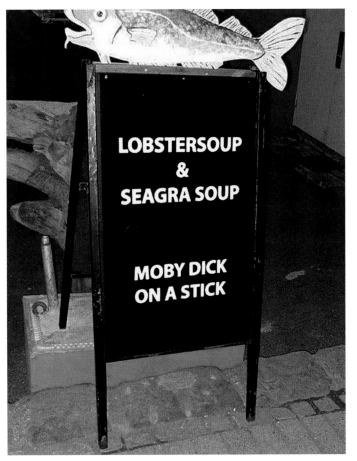

Reykjavik, Iceland

Enter the belly of the beast

Florence, Italy

UN peacekeepers were sent in to relieve Americano drinkers

Trondheim, Norway

The plaice for Motown flavour

Sheffield, UK

 *Like this*

Bursa, Turkey

Easy on the ketchup,
heavy on the puns

Blackpool, UK

The ultimate knock-off cuisine

Geneva, Switzerland

Includes the classic hit dish Bohemian Anchovy

London, UK

Warning: Hot spice.
Not for pussies

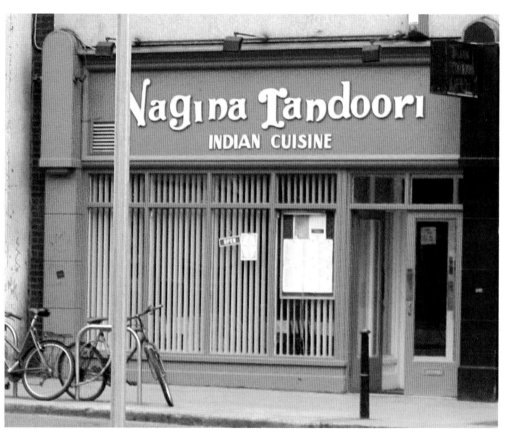

Dublin, Ireland

But treat her right

.Cape Breton Island, Canada

Not Number One

Toronto, Canada

*Vietnamese has never been
so gangsta*

Cambridge, Canada

A chance eating

Toronto, Canada

Flame grilled and disastrously good

Toronto, Canada

Prepared by hand

Wilsonville, OR, USA

You'll never share a table again
(because they have none)

Bluffton, SC, USA

It's been emotional . . .

Greensboro, NC, USA

Avoid the iceberg lettuce

Washington DC, USA

Made fresh daily

Ocean City, NJ, USA

Chef's Tip:
Quit lookin' at him funny

New York, NY, USA

The perfect comfort break

Tipton, IN, USA

Can we eat it?
YES WE CAN!

Weeksville, NY, USA

The Lord grills in mysterious ways

Fort Worth, TX, USA

Put fire in your belly

Cambridge, MA, USA

Hot dog tastes great

Austin, TX, USA

Chicks with attitude

Washington DC, USA

Your dinner

Rosemead, CA, USA

The biggest dumplings around

Portland, OR, USA

Eat here and you'll never grow up!

New York, NY, USA

Serves only 100% Chinese pork

New York, NY, USA

Something smells fishy in here

Ocean City, NJ, USA

And the Best Hot Dog goes to . . .
you. And you. And you . . .

Los Angeles, CA, USA

You won't know what hit you

Atlanta, GA, USA

Stuff your poker face

Miami, FL, USA

Hot dogs you can believe in

Miami, FL, USA

Eat fast (food), die young

Morrisville, VT, USA

Managing customer expectation since 1972

Los Angeles, CA, USA

Sushi to warm your heart

Portland, OR, USA

A latte energy in the morning

Westmont, IL, USA

You'll keep coming back for more . . .

Butler, PA, USA

Winner of the 2012 Good Taste Awards

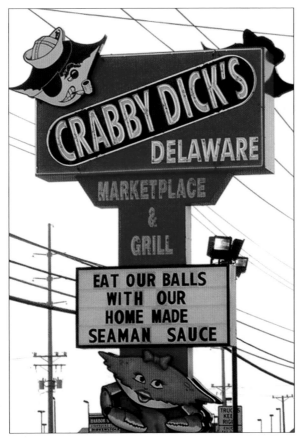

Rehoboth Beach, DE, USA

Margaritas with morals

Ocean City, NJ, USA

Children must be supervised by an adult (at all times)

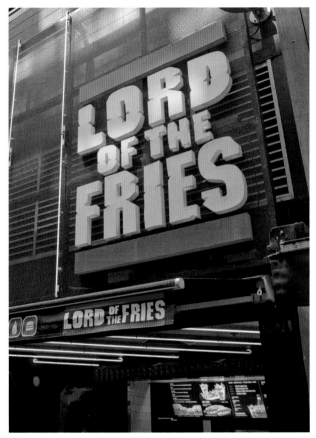

Melbourne, Australia

Medium, rare or extinct

Sydney, Australia

Brides-to-go

Sydney, Australia

Green Curry: the perfect date bait

EN Thai Sing
Thai Restaurant
Eat in - Take away
9344 - 0099

Terrigal, Australia

A great gastro pub

Nairobi, Kenya

High-minded dining

Okankolo, Namibia

*So that's where Osama
was hiding . . .*

Okankolo, Namibia

The birds and the bees – over lunch

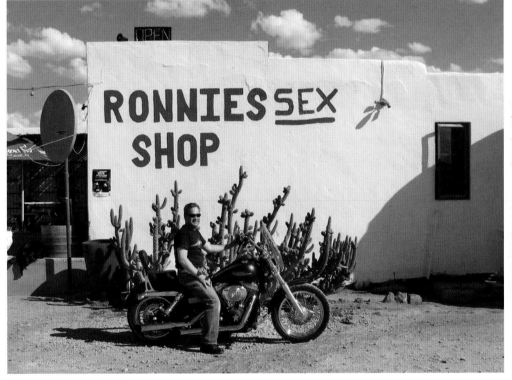

Swellendam, South Africa

Mayor of London HQ

Kochi, India

King of Mince

Mumbai, India

Grand Tofu Master of the Universe

Bean curd person of high skill

Huwei, Taiwan

Don't expect them to get your order right

Taipei, Taiwan

*If it's good enough for Goldilocks,
it's good enough for you*

小馋熊美食
LITTLE DROOLING BEAR FOOD

岐山臊子面
¥10

陈皮红豆汤
¥6

腊汁肉夹馍
¥5/个

Shanghai, China

Full address still pending

Hong Kong, China

Now with plumbing at each table

Taipei, Taiwan

You won't feel, or taste, a thing

Lijiang, China

So why not give it to him?
(He'll taste better)

The fish wants the sauce to eat

Taipei, Taiwan

Aromatic, full-flavoured blends also available

Xi'an, China

Food with a happy ending

Shanghai, China

Inewitable gweat food

MY FAVOR STEAK

麦菲尔扒王

Kunming, China

Prices that won't ruin you

Phnom Penh, Cambodia

Do <u>not</u> upset the waitress

Osaka, Japan

Even the gravy exudes charisma

Tokyo, Japan

*When the weight of the world
is just too much . . .*

Kyoto, Japan

There's no need to feel down

Kyoto, Japan

Eye-wateringly good food

牛丼 かつ丼

BEEF BAWL

Tokyo, Japan

'Big Yac and fries, please'

Kagbeni, Nepal

Raised to be dinner

Seoul, South Korea

The Bucks stop here

Gyeongsangbuk-do, South Korea

Breakfast? Whatever . . .

Busan, South Korea

Where pigs go 'moo'

Uijeongbu, South Korea

You bring the beef,
I'll bring the swine

Singapore

Always wash your hands
<u>after</u> you eat

Phuket, Thailand

All your needs for a good night out

Chiang Mai, Thailand

Don't miss the glazed donuts

Phi Phi Islands, Thailand

Acknowledgements

I would like to thank the following people for providing photographs. Without you, this book would not have been possible.

Jamie Palmer, Chris Stoddart, Christian Cable, Johnnie Packington, Tom Page-Phillips, Thomas Guest, Ross MacPherson, Kim Bülow Bonfils, Michael Shepherd, Doug Newton, Gill Theaker, Jeremy Markowitz, Mark Norman Francis, Steve Mannion, Keely Richardson, Heather Rai, Bill Kennedy, Fred McElwaine, Kristina Thimm, Patrick Smith, http://www.askthepilot.com, Anton Zafereo, Vinayak Hegde, Erhan Erdoğan, Jesse Russell, Esmond Yau, Stephen Wray, Andrew Nguyen, Patrick Tanguay, Martyn Weir, Matt Richardson, Dianne Krone, Chris Bullneck, Jeremy Schultz, Victor Tate Photography www.asaltandbattery.com, David Cory, Nelson Wan, Lance Eckels, Ahmet Ziyaeddin, Catherine Ling, Elliot Cheung, Jeremiah Allen, Jerry Abstract, Mark K, Renee Huang, Saul Blumenthal, Linus Lee, Tony Singh, Turner Wright, Elise Bernard, Jon Racasa, Bruce Fingerhood, Rachael McCurdy, Henry Ho, Patricia S. Greenstein, Daphne Chong, David Myers, David Mallozzi, Eric Steuer, Becky Houtman, Michael Bruchas, Stephanie Steele, Bill Trenwith, scottamus on Flickr, Sam Koronczyk, Nari Clarke, Ashok Hariharan, Dan Rosenberg, Danie van der Merwe, Karon Liu, William James Tychonievich, Thomas Scherber, Will Gee, Aram Armstrong, Robert Rabinowitz, Will Burns, Troy Parsons, Stefan I., Trishan Panch (www.hybridvigour.net), Carianne Carleo-Evangelist, David Lewinnek, Nathan Wales, Camemberu.com, Peter Cuce, Nils Trebing, Emily S. Lee, D. Müller, Marie McClellan, Cheng "hellaOAKLAND", Mohamed Salim, Tanya Procyshyn, Jeremiah Roth, Sarah Blythe, Tom Bromwich, Marissa Chen, Joe Brooke, Lily Faber, Lesley Faber, Penguin Press crew, David Walker, Nick Hill, Nicky Palmer, Mark Ollard, Matt Clacher, Jess Kim, Lija Kresowaty, Caroline Craig, Jo Davy (www.davy.co.uk).

I am greatly indebted to the brilliant Charlotte Humphery, who superbly assembled the book, and spent many an afternoon banging her head against her desk helping to come up with captions. To Gesche Ipsen, Marissa Chen, Kyle McEnery and everyone at Penguin, thank you for your help and suggestions. I am very grateful also to Keith Taylor, Hannah Bradbury, Gill Heeley and Andrew Smith for expertly steering, producing and designing the book. Most of all, I would like to thank Lily Faber: your humour, kindness and patience know no bounds – especially when we were walking around London together taking pictures of restaurants like 'Vijay' in sub-zero temperatures.